Carl

Love Nana Sweet

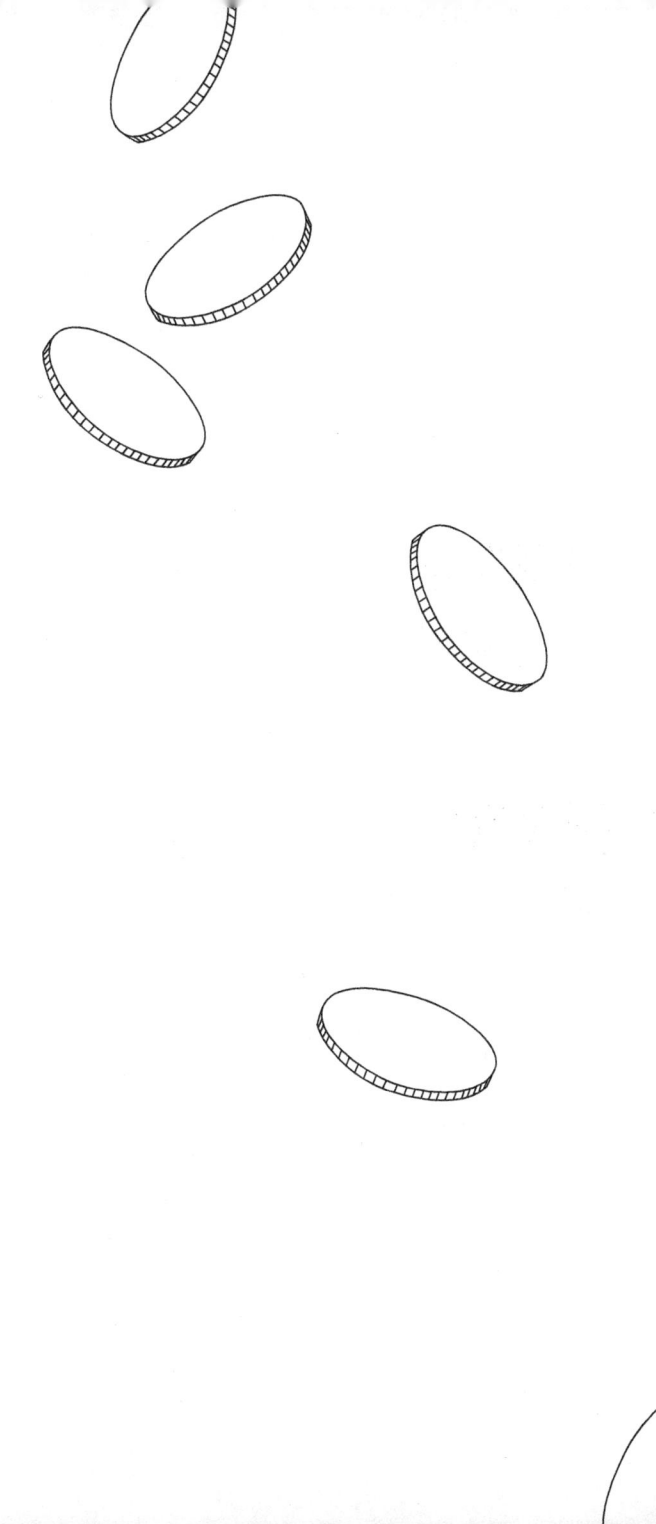

Money Smarts
for Teens & Twenties

Understanding why financial planning works, makes it easy!

Gordon Hughes, CFP

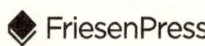

Suite 300 - 990 Fort St
Victoria, BC, V8V 3K2
Canada

www.friesenpress.com

Copyright © 2019 by Gordon Hughes
First Edition — 2019

All rights reserved.

No part of this publication may be reproduced in any form, or by any means, electronic or mechanical, including photocopying, recording, or any information browsing, storage, or retrieval system, without permission in writing from FriesenPress.

ISBN
978-1-5255-2504-9 (Hardcover)
978-1-5255-2505-6 (Paperback)
978-1-5255-2506-3 (eBook)

1. BUSINESS & ECONOMICS, PERSONAL FINANCE, MONEY MANAGEMENT

Distributed to the trade by The Ingram Book Company

Written for teenagers but can be a helpful resource for parents, teachers, and other adults.

The Author says:

As a financial planner, I've seen the sad results of people blindly starting out in life without the simple basic understanding about finances. I believe young people are very capable of success and happiness. All they need is to be informed. This book offers some things to do, other things to avoid, and why.

Table of Contents

Chapter One The Beginning Is Now!........................... 9
True financial freedom means not worrying about money. The choices you make today do impact your life, both now and in the future. If you could save yourself ten to twelve years of work in the future, have more time for fun and not have it cost you anything now, wouldn't that be great? You can!

Chapter Two Time vs. Money: Which Is Worth More? 15
We look at the real cost of a $10,000 car. This side-by-side comparison of two choices demonstrates how much one car really costs. Learn a better way.

Chapter Three More Secrets of a Happy Life 27
Develop self-worth from within instead of boosting your ego with material things.

Chapter Four What Might Steal Your Wealth?.......... 39
At thirty years old, Colleen reviews her life and looks back at her mistakes. After a few quick calculations she realizes how a simple change in her lifestyle will pay off. She realizes how

she was sucked in by big business ads. She also learns a way to gain a million dollars.

Chapter Five Where Do We Go from Here?............. 45
Some Tips to get started. Some suggestions on how to become your own person, become wealthy, and have friends who support and affirm you.

Chapter One
The Beginning Is Now!

Some adults have to work almost all their lives. Others get to stop working sooner. They take up hobbies and interests they enjoy. They enjoy their freedom longer and the difference began while they were young. Some have fun enjoying an extra ten to fifteen years of retirement.

I owe, I owe, it's off to work I go.

You don't get to decide at age forty-five to quit work unless you plan ahead. Many people can't afford to retire early and are trapped into having to work longer. Some people are able to retire early but choose to work because they love their work, but those people know they have the financial freedom to choose.

Let's learn how to play the game of financial freedom.

You will learn to recognize who your opponents are as we go.

The object of the game is freedom. Do you want to be free to choose for yourself? Of course you do, as long as it doesn't mean having less enjoyment now, right?

What if you could do everything you want to do now and still be free to have fun for an extra ten years of your life?

There are a few simple secrets to enjoying life both now and later. By knowing these secrets you'll be able to make better choices for yourself and get what you really want in life.

Check out these choices—which do you prefer?

> **A)** Work forty hours a week for an extra ten to twenty years just to pay off bills.

OR

> **B)** Be free to retire young and do what you want for the rest of your life.

The Beginning Is Now!

travel? *play sports?*

Money Smarts for Teens & Twenties

Imagine you are age fifty and you don't have to work anymore to pay bills or earn an income to support your living expenses. If money was no object, what would you want to do with your life? Write down your dreams here.

The Beginning Is Now!

_____

_____

_____

_____

_____

_____

It's up to you.

Frequently Asked Questions

Q. Why must I decide now?
A. To retire early you need to prepare early. It's not automatic.

Q. Is it hard to do?
A. Not if you really understand how it works. You'll have some attractive benefits by preparing properly.

Chapter Two
Time vs. Money: Which Is Worth More?

Salespeople and businesses make money when you buy their products. Advertising can persuade you to spend your money. They win when they sell stuff to you. You transfer your wealth to those merchants. You are helping them get rich.

Many teens have no idea how to buy things. No one has shown them the true cost of spending. The cost of payback is the first secret to learn on your path to financial freedom.

Handling money is like a game. Freedom is the prize for those who learn to play the game well. In this game, your opponents are not always obvious. Some of your opponents, like attractive ads and professionally designed displays, make it easy for you to choose to spend, even if the item is not really needed.

You need to understand what you'll need to do now and in the future to pay for each purchase. If you use credit to buy something, don't forget about the interest you will need

Money Smarts for Teens & Twenties

to pay in the future. Sometimes the credit card interest can double the amount you actually pay for a purchase. Knowing this enables you to be able to make a better decision. But that's not the end of the story.

You win when you buy things that enhance your life now and in the future. You lose when you are lured to buy something that won't serve you in the long term. Buy well.

Using money smarts now will equip you to travel the world one day if you wish. One goal is to avoid the pressures exerted by businesses and by peers. Your peers may have already been persuaded by advertising to spend their money. Ads are everywhere: online, on your phone, TV, magazines, billboards, and more. Ads are designed to change your thinking so companies can get some of your money. Brainwashing people with advertising really works for their game plan. They advertise so much you think you want to buy their stuff. When they do this, they win and you give up a piece of your freedom.

Companies make it easy for people to buy now and pay later. That's one of their tricks in this game of wealth. They want you to not just transfer your wealth to them for the item you bought, they also entice you to make payments that collect interest, which transfers another part of your future freedom to them.

Borrowing money to buy something now with the promise to pay later limits your future. Credit is not always a bad thing, but you need to become aware of how it works before it's too late for you. Misuse of credit can lead to

Time vs. Money: Which Is Worth More?

bankruptcy when the interest load becomes too great to handle.

The second secret is to understand the length of time you have to work to pay for today's purchases. It can take the fun out of buying new things just to have them. Beware of the other team's buy-now-pay-later strategy.

The third secret is that your payback doesn't stop at the end of the loan. If it was only the amount you see on paper it would be bad enough, but a hasty, unnecessary purchase can have consequences far beyond just the money you pay for something.

The following example will show you the real cost of a used car.

Jason and Brittany are both twenty years old. They earn the same wages. They are both single, and both have similar living expenses. The difference is one buys a car and the other doesn't.

Jason is attracted to a sports car on the used car lot. This car is a few years old, and he believes he was smart to negotiate with the salesperson to lower the sticker price from $12,000 to $10,000.

Jason gets the $10,000 price and is proud of his financial savvy. After all, he did save $2,000 by bargaining and he figures, that has got to be good, right? We'll see.

Money Smarts for Teens & Twenties

Jason signs an agreement to purchase the car on credit and will pay $229 a month for five years to pay off the $10,000 and the loan interest and sales tax. Now he has a nice-looking, shiny sports car to drive!

Brittany doesn't buy a car, and already she has more freedom. Her freedom is in knowing that she isn't obligated to make any payments for five years.

Basically, Jason has made a five-year commitment to pay for his car loan. If Jason stops paying the loan, the financial institution will repossess his car. This could also be considered a sentence to debtor's prison, because it took away some of his freedom. Jason must work to pay the loan. He really doesn't have the liberty to stop work unless he sells the car and pays off his loan.

> Today we don't have debtor's prisons but there is a penalty for those who frequently or repeatedly lose at this money game. In a hockey game the penalty box is for the individual who must

Time vs. Money: Which Is Worth More?

> stop playing for a time. In the credit game a spender may be forced to stop buying due to no more credit available. This spiral starts in a small way by just spending every dollar you earn. Soon people begin to borrow money from others to buy things.

Jason spends money on car insurance, gas, and car maintenance such as oil changes, tires and repairs.

Brittany spends the same amount on bus fares, occasional taxi rides, and several times a year she rents a car for road trips.

These car expenses for Jason and the taxis and buses for Brittany even out. They both spend the same amount each month; with only one exception—Jason's car payment.

Brittany doesn't have to make those payments. Jason does.

Brittany decides to invest $229 monthly (the same amount Jason pays on his car loan) out of her paycheck. By investing she not only saves that money, she also earns interest on her savings. Wait till you see what Jason really paid for that car!

> Prison work gangs were used in the old days to force prisoners to work hard for no pay as punishment for their crimes. Jason's credit work gang is of his own choosing.

Money smart people discover alternatives to buying things. That way they don't have to work hard to pay for past purchases.

Money smart people prefer to be in charge of their own time. They aren't manipulated by advertising or peer pressure. They spend time playing and following their dreams as well as working.

They live their dreams like skiing, painting a picture, writing a poem, playing a musical instrument, playing sports, travelling the world, doing charity work, and much more. Many of these interests don't have to cost a lot of money either. Money smart people compare and shop for alternatives even when they are engaged in a hobby.

Some people work so hard that they have little time for friends and family. Some are so rushed they seem to always be tired and grouchy due to stress. If your folks are like this, don't blame them— probably no one ever taught them these secrets of wealth.

Back to the car—let's see the real cost of buying on credit.

Time vs. Money: Which Is Worth More?

COMPARE

Age 20

Jason buys a car.

He pays $10,000 + sales tax. Total $11,600. He pays $229 a month for 5 years.

Brittany has no car.

She invests $229 monthly for 5 years.

Age 25

Jason has a rusty car.

Jason spends $300 a month on gas, oil, tires, insurance, etc.

Brittany has $16,625.

Brittany spends $300 a month on taxis, buses and car rentals.

Both Jason and Brittany stop the $229 a month payments at age 25. Brittany's investments grow as interest is added. Watch what happens next!

NOTE: Brittany is not adding any more money to her investment. The growth is just the return on her investment being added to her savings.

Age 30

Jason has a memory of a rusty old car.

Brittany has $23,317.

Age 35

Jason has a memory of a rusty old car.

Brittany has $ 32,704.

Age 40

Jason has a memory of a rusty old car.

Brittany has $ 45,869.

Age 45

Jason has a faded memory of a rusty old car.

Brittany has $64,334.

Brittany and Jason have used their money in exactly the same way from age twenty-five onward. Neither of them added anything to their savings. Both of them spent 100% of their income in this example. Was it really worth $64,334 for Jason to buy his $10,000 car? He paid $229 for 60 months just to own that car.

NOTE: The $64,334.is calculated using a 7% rate.

If Jason wants to catch up to Brittany in savings, how many years will he have to work to save an extra $64,334?

Time vs. Money: Which Is Worth More?

In order to do this, Jason must save that money in addition to paying for his everyday living expenses. To even try to catch up to Brittany he'll probably have to work two jobs.

Assume that Brittany doesn't touch her invested money for twenty more years. This allows her money to grow and we really notice the magic of the compounding of interest.

Britany will have $248,951 by age 65, so Jason has 20 years to save $248,951. He will need to save $490 a month for 20 years at 7%.

> Compound interest is when your savings earns interest for one year. Then you leave both the savings plus the interest to earn more interest. Now your interest is earning more interest; that's called compounding. Let it grow long enough and your annual interest earned can become larger than the original savings you started with!

That magic of compound interest gets bigger the longer you leave it there.

Age 50

Jason has a faded memory of a rusty old car.

Brittany has $ 90,231.

Age 55

Jason has a faded memory of a rusty old car.

Brittany has $ 126,554.

Age 60

Jason has a faded memory of a rusty old car.

Brittany has $ 177,499.

Age 65

Jason has completely forgotten his rusty old car.

Brittany has $ 248,951.

Amazing how much that $10,000 used car really cost Jason in his future!

To calculate the difference in rates of return you need to know about the rule of 72. This rule will give you an estimate of how each interest rate will perform. You simply divide the interest rate into the number 72 and that gives you the approximate number of years it takes to double your money.

For example: 2% return being divided into 72 shows us it takes about thirty-six years to double your money. For our math example let's use $1 invested in the beginning. We are looking at a period from age twenty to age sixty-five, or forty-five years.

So, $1.00 invested at 2% would yield about $2.50 total.

Let's look at 7%. Dividing 7 into 72 tells us that $1 will double every ten years.

Let's follow it through for forty-five years. $1 becomes $2 in ten years. Then it doubles again to become $4 in twenty years. $4 becomes $8 in thirty years; $16 in forty

Time vs. Money: Which Is Worth More?

years; and approximately $20 at the forty-five-year mark. What a difference!

Now compare with 10%. It will double every 7 years.

$1 becomes $2 in seven years; $4 in fourteen years; $8 in twenty-one years; $16 in twenty-eight years; $32 in thirty-five years; $64 in forty-two years; $128 in forty-nine years; $256 in fifty-six years. So, at year forty-five we'll estimate it to be around $85..

It is good to follow each year regardless of how repetitive it seems. Note that 10% produced about eight times as much as 7%. This is not what most people assume to be true because they don't typically think beyond simple math. Note any investment that returns a higher rate also has a greater risk of losing money!

Don't be lured too quickly into high return investments. Start with low interest deposits until you have the equivalent of three months' living expenses. A basic bank account can serve at this level. There is no need to complicate things just yet.

After you have three months' expenses saved you may look at other opportunities. Never put 100% of your savings in investments that promise higher returns. Get yourself a qualified financial advisor. Check for credentials like CFP or equivalent. Just don't do direct investing online until you have a good understanding of the risks and rewards involved.

Financial Freedom begins with lifestyle choices—so does bankruptcy!

Chapter Three
More Secrets of a Happy Life

Jason had no idea what he would have to give up in life to buy that car. If he'd only known the real cost in time and effort! Keeping this a secret helps companies and merchandisers win at the money game. If you want to win at this game you need to become aware of the real cost of every purchase in life.

One great secret of becoming wealthy is to uncover the real cost by looking ahead. Put each buying decision to the test. Here are a few questions to help:

1. Am I buying this just to impress others, maybe with a certain brand name?
2. Will it really serve me well in the future?
3. Am I buying this because I want to feel better by buying something?

Money Smarts for Teens & Twenties

If the answer to the third question is yes, then tell a guidance counsellor or other adult how you feel. There are better ways to deal with feelings than spending money. Empower yourself from within. Empowerment generates a feeling of satisfaction in your own accomplishments.

If I want to feel different than I do at this moment I must ask myself what can I do to improve my feelings. Fools look for instant gratification.

Wise people look beyond the moment and make constructive changes. Positive changes will benefit you for a lifetime. Whether it's money management or managing your feelings, it's best to not reach for instant gratification. Planning ahead really pays off big time!

The power to change is within you.

You can feel good without buying status items. In fact, you may even feel better knowing you have grown beyond the need to own things just to feel good. Financial freedom rewards those who look beyond the present to see the full picture.

The richest person in a room isn't the one with the most money. The richest person is the one with the least wants. Think about this. The one with the most wants is never happy or satisfied because they always want something they don't have. If you want what you already have and are grateful for that, you will tend to move toward financial freedom.

As a financial planner, I meet people who have small incomes and are very happy and content. They feel very secure without large amounts of income. They enjoy their

More Secrets of a Happy Life

family, their modest home, and their health. They love one another and feel part of their community. Money itself cannot buy freedom from worry and stress.

I've also met people with large incomes who worry so much about material things like furniture, cars, appearances, business deals, and their investments that they miss out on some important aspects of life. They seem to always be in a rush. They may be wealthy with money, but not so rich in happiness. As my mother used to say, "The best things in life are free!"

Some people miss the quiet security that comes from not needing things to make them feel good. Lack of money doesn't mean serenity every time. There are people who have little money that do worry a lot, and are not so content. There are also wealthy people who are secure and content.

The point is that happiness is not tied to money or the lack of it. Happiness comes from dealing with our own thoughts and feelings. No amount of money can buy happiness.

Money Smarts for Teens & Twenties

It's not having money that creates a problem in life. It's the love of money that is the root of all evil. One can be very poor financially and still love money. Poor folk who envy those that have money are generally unhappy too. Accepting who you are and being grateful for what you have is a great place to start in achieving happiness.

Another secret to a happy life is to give to others. When we care enough about others to give them something they need, then we feel like a true friend. Giving to others helps you feel good about yourself. Only give if it is a gift of love or caring.

When giving is done from a sincere heart and not just to impress someone, our gifts are usually appreciated and our friendships grow. I can't explain it, but the universe seems to return to us what we give to others. That seems to happen whether we are mean or loving. Giving just to feel good or to impress people usually backfires. Try to give for the right reason, which is to help someone or to share in a celebration or overcome a tragedy in their lives.

Back to the purchase: Once you've decided there is good reason to buy something, do one more thing. Ask: Is this the right time to buy it?

You may want to buy it if you have enough money and still have money left over. If you plan to buy now and pay later, then reread about Jason's car purchase.

What will it really cost you? Is it really worth it? Can you get the same benefit in a less expensive way? Can you rent it? Can you share with someone else? Think the options and benefits through to the end.

More Secrets of a Happy Life

The costs are not just financial. The emotional pressure of paying for unnecessary material things can and does destroy relationships and seriously impacts lives. If you prefer peace of mind and no worries, just look ahead. If you can use some money smarts now, you will be better able to avoid money hassles later. Stress and worry are not fun.

Jason wanted the good feeling that he got from cruising the streets in his shiny new car. He wanted to come and go when he pleased. What he didn't know was that he would have to give up so much freedom for the rest of his life for a bit of fun now. If he'd only known, he might have made a wiser financial decision, like Brittany did.

Here's another secret to feeling good that doesn't take money.

"Some people are prepared to do without what others have now so they can have later on what others cannot." One of my teachers, Mel, used this quote often. I don't know who he was quoting, but it's true.

When we think owning a new bike, car, dress, shoes, iPod, or cell phone will make us feel better about ourselves, we need to think twice.

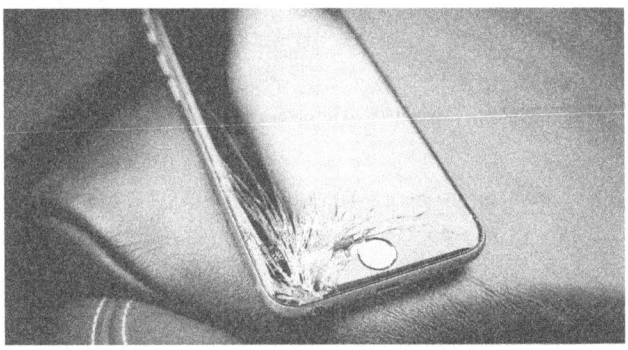

Buy things that will have a genuine use in your life, not just because someone else has one.

Becoming an adult is rewarding and exciting. When we understand how today's decisions affect our future, life is even more abundant. Knowing you are making the best choices possible gives you a sense of pride and security. It's a similar feeling of pride Jason felt when he bought his car except your feeling of pride comes from within and doesn't cost you years of regret.

Jason made his decision based on the knowledge he had at the time and he felt good about it, but that feeling was short-lived and he paid for it the rest of his life. It is to the advantage of big business to keep people uninformed about the true cost, as people who are trapped by their own commitments to payments pressures them to be loyal employees.

You need to become an individual, not just follow the crowd. An individual doesn't need shiny things, brand name clothes, or big toys to feel good. Individuals learn to feel good about themselves, because they become aware that their self-worth doesn't depend upon their net worth or a display of things they own.

Self-worth doesn't depend on net worth.

Self-worth is the true feeling that I'm as good as anyone else. I don't need to show off to get attention, and I don't feel insecure or inferior about myself. I don't need to prove anything to my peers for their approval.

More Secrets of a Happy Life

> Net worth is what is left after you sell everything you own and pay off all your bills. It's just a measure of your material stuff.

Jason's story continues

There is still more payback for Jason's decision!

Jason decides at age forty-five that he wants to save money to retire at age fifty-five. He will need to catch up to Brittany in order to do this.

Q. How much must Jason save to catch up to Brittany?
A. He must accumulate $126,554 by age fifty-five to catch up to Brittany.

Q. How much extra must Jason save every month to accumulate $126,554 in ten years?
A. He must save over $750 every month from age forty-five to age fifty-five to catch up. That's nearly $9,000. every year for 10 years!

In addition, Jason must live. He must pay all living expenses to run his home and feed his family. Plus, he must also save as much as Brittany is saving during that ten-year period to keep from losing ground.

Do you think he will be able to do all that on the exact same income as Brittany? Of course not! He'll have to work two jobs—this is more debtor's prison payback.

Is it mission impossible for Jason? Do you think Jason had any clue what he was sacrificing just to drive that car when he was a young man?

Money Smarts for Teens & Twenties

Q. Did anyone ever explain the future costs to Jason?
A. No! That's the merchant's secret. That's how they make fortunes at the expense of unsuspecting buyers. Merchandisers often win at the money game because buyers don't think through to the consequences.

Q. If Jason had understood the true costs in addition to the mere payments, would he have bought that car?
A. Probably not. But if someone had only given him the financial impact information, at least he would have known ahead of time.

There are times when it isn't convenient to postpone a purchase like buying a car. Perhaps you live in an area where there are no bus services. Maybe such considerations make it seem nearly impossible to postpone. Let's look again at the figures. Between age fifty-five and age sixty-five, Brittany's investment gained about $125,000 at 7%. Yes, sixty-five is a long way off, but there are people who are still very active and healthy at that age who would like to travel the world or do other things that cost money.

If this is your situation, can you carpool with someone who works at the same place or at nearby workplace? Would it be an option to move closer to work, or find work closer to home? Some jobs require you to use a company vehicle, if so, are you allowed to take it home after work? Working handier to home may cut down on travelling time, save gas, and allow

More Secrets of a Happy Life

you to have more personal time. A lower wage can sometimes be the wiser choice.

The earlier you begin savings and investing the grater the return.

If you have the ability to borrow larger sums, you can use other people's money to your advantage. I have designed the Smart Choice Life Plan, which is a Life Plan that can outperform Registered Education Plans and Registered Retirement Savings Plans but must be done according to investments with guarantees and using periodic investments to greatly reduce risk. I have a PowerPoint program which is available to your financial advisor if they sell the products needed to build this program.

What a price we pay for today's purchases. Had someone shown Jason that his car would cost him the price of a modest home, and even that by working another ten years he cannot make up for the deficit in his bank account, Jason wouldn't be able to blame anyone for how he spent his money. If only he had known the impact ahead of time.

Jason still can't blame anyone else, since the people in his life probably weren't given this information either. This has been a very well-kept secret for generations by the establishment. By the establishment, I mean our whole materialistic society.

If it was profitable for businesses to know about this side of the money game it would be front and centre. It isn't profitable for them, so advertisers keep it hidden to make it easier for you to open your purse and give them your wealth.

Businesses profit at the expense of the Jasons of this world. The car dealer won by making money off the car he sold. The bank won because it made money from the loan Jason used to buy the car. The people Jason works for also win because they have a trained employee who can't choose to retire because he is still paying for the mistakes of his youth. They don't have to spend money training someone else to do his job.

Proper purchasing might take more money smarts and constraint than some teenagers can muster. But when you're armed with the knowledge that Jason was missing you can choose the quality of life for yourself.

I have every faith that teenagers are just as smart and just as wise as anyone at any age. What they are missing is the knowledge that experience teaches. We gain experience by making mistakes as well as doing well in life and observing others.

"Smart people learn from their own mistakes. Wise people learn from the mistakes of others."

Q. Why would some young adults still be tempted to buy a car even after reading this book?
A. They might want to feel important because they have a shiny car. It boosts their status among their peers. This is tempting. They may also have a genuine need to own a car to travel to university or work, especially if they live in a rural area. It would be wise to thoroughly explore all options, busses, ride sharing etc. before making the purchase.

People in their forties, fifties, and sixties still buy shiny toys like cars and boats, and build oversized homes just to show off their status. So we would expect young people to follow their example of materialism, unless they know better.

More Secrets of a Happy Life

Whether you are age sixteen or sixty-one, if you haven't learned something on your own and no one ever taught you, then you don't know it. Many older adults still don't have a clue as to how much they were manipulated by advertising, peer pressure, and personal pride to buy things unwisely.

Try to find wisdom now, so you'll be able to enjoy things in life that others cannot. In a coffee shop newsletter I saw the following quote, "Wisdom comes with age, but sometimes age comes alone." If you learn all you can about life experiences, you can be wise at any age.

> **Money Smarts:** Financial Freedom starts with lifestyle choices—so does bankruptcy!

Chapter Four
What Might Steal Your Wealth?

Colleen had the weekend off and was home alone. She looked forward to this time for herself. Her kids went to their grandparents' for the weekend. Greg, her husband, had gone fishing with two of his pals. This was a treat to be home alone with nothing to do and she planned to enjoy it.

On their back deck, Colleen decided to soak up the sun and catch up on reading her magazines. She lit up a cigarette, helped herself to a cold glass of pop, and checked her emails before starting to read.

Soon after she stretched out on her hammock she realized the glare of the sun reflecting off her magazine took the joy out of reading. So, she tossed the magazines aside, lit another cigarette, and sipped on the still cool pop.

She began thinking about her family's struggle to meet expenses and provide for the children. She took one last drag of her cigarette and tried to relax. She was almost asleep when her package of cigarettes dropped to the deck and caught her attention. While she bent over to pick up her pack she wondered how much smoking costs her. She got up and took a pen and a pad of paper and began to calculate how much she had spent over the years.

Colleen thought she was grown-up enough to smoke when she was twelve years old. She started smoking an occasional cigarette to fit in and be cool. How childish that seemed to her today at age thirty. Did she really think that smoking a cigarette made her look cool? Why did she think that a cigarette was stylish? Was it because of TV ads or was it peer pressure?

She started smoking in the days before health warnings were printed on the packages. In those days there were ads showing glamorous women holding cigarettes and there were also girls with athletic youthful appearances in cigarette ads. Big business had really lured her in with those ads. *I wish I'd known then what I know now*, Colleen thought with regret.

When Colleen was twelve, she only bought about a pack a month. The next year she got a part-time job and started

What Might Steal Your Wealth?

buying about two packs a week for the next two years. Then she increased to a pack a day.

When Colleen started smoking, cigarettes cost about $3.75 a pack; now they are nearly $10.00. It's easy to see why most people don't smoke so much any more.

Here are Colleen's calculations:
$3.75 x 12 packs = $45.00 that first year
$4.00 x 2 packs a week x 52 weeks = 416.00 the second year
$4.50 x 2 packs a week x 52 weeks = $468.00 the third year
$5.00 x 7 packs a week x 52 = $1,820 every year by the time Colleen was age fifteen

She remembered how hard it had been to keep her supply of cigarettes that winter. It was OK while she was working extra hours in the summer, but during the school year it was really hard.

Colleen is now age thirty. Fifteen years ago, cigarettes cost $5.00 a pack and they are now $10.00, so for her calculations she took an average of $7.50.

$7.50 x 365 days = $2,737.50 a year multiplied by 15 years = $ 41,062.50

Colleen was stunned. *That's what I spent on cigarettes the past fifteen years?*

"Wow! That's a lot of money! That's more than the price of a new car! We could've bought two cars like the one we own now. Boy-oh-boy was I fooled by those ads! Now it's so hard to quit!" Colleen felt trapped.

What a fool she felt she was. Colleen thought, *Thank God I never got the notion that drinking and doing drugs was cool. People who got lured into the drug habit must have wasted a fortune! No wonder they call it being wasted. They become so dependent on drugs they can't live without their dope. What a terrible life that must be, being a slave to a drug!*

Those pill pushers and drug dealers make a huge fortune off suckers like that, she thought as she reached for her pack of cigarettes. That's when it struck her. She was just as hooked on smokes as someone who was hooked on alcohol or cocaine.

I, Colleen, am as hooked on nicotine as they are on their drugs and alcohol, otherwise I would just quit! My habit only costs $10 a day and theirs is probably $100 a day or more. God help them.

Colleen put down the pack of cigarettes and picked up the pad and pen again. She figured if cigarettes cost $10 now and never went up in price again, she would spend $3,650 a year. If cigarettes don't kill her and she lives to age sixty-five, that'll cost her $3,650 x 35 years = $127,750.

> Entertainment is good, but beware of anything addictive. The cost in dollars is huge and some pay the ultimate costs in loss of health and even death. Addictions are great blocks to financial freedom.

The price has more than doubled in the past fifteen years. *I was going to just enjoy the weekend, now I start thinking about this. I'd better try to quit. There is no better time than today,* Colleen thought. She threw her pack of cigarettes away.

What Might Steal Your Wealth?

Still amazed by the expense, Colleen reflected on how easily she and other young people got drawn in by big business. Advertising never told her about the real cost of smoking. Neither had her parents or her teachers calculated the financial cost with her. Were they all in the dark? Colleen wondered if the younger generation today is any better informed than her generation was back then. She certainly hopes they are.

Colleen has a program on her computer that can add up the real cost of her habit and help inform her children to help them avoid such mistakes because of lack of detailed information.

She entered a $3,650 deposit into an investment for the first year. That was what it cost her every year to smoke now. She set the annual increase at only 5% to allow for increase in the price of cigarettes going up like they always have.

Next, she calculated if a person at age twenty smoked a pack a day, what they would spend up to age sixty-five. Many smokers die before age sixty-five as a result of their smoking, but some would live beyond that.

She also wanted to figure an investment of that money with 8% on average for forty-five years, so she keyed in an interest rate of 8%.

So here goes ... she hit the calculate button. Holy smokes! The total is $3,013,717! What could a person do with three million dollars?

Money Smarts for Teens & Twenties

Not much wonder those large companies try to tempt young people and keep them in the dark. Look at the profits they'll make from their victims!

Colleen thought she would do one more calculation based on a 6% return on investments. $1,849,228; wow! That's still nearly two million dollars wasted on cigarettes.

How many teens have been informed about this? Has anyone told them that by not following the crowd they might enjoy much more freedom?

"Boy, I wish I was age twenty and know what I know now!" Colleen laments again.

Colleen thought, *I believe that if teachers and parents put the whole truth in front of teens, most of them have the wisdom to make great decisions. It's just that corporate greed has done such a great job of manipulating the thinking of everyone, not just our youth. My parents love me and would have shared this information if anyone had shown them.*

Think about the perceived benefits, since most of the things we get entrapped in are really due to our low self-image. Colleen can't think of a single real benefit of smoking today, but she can list dozens of advantages of not smoking.

Money Smarts: Whether it's addictions or just buying the latest clothing styles or gadget on the market that gets us in trouble, it won't fix our image of ourselves in any lasting way. When considering your next purchase, always take time to ponder the real results and weigh out whether the true cost is worth the perceived benefits.

Money Smarts: Financial Freedom begins with lifestyle choices—so does bankruptcy!

Chapter Five
Where Do We Go from Here?

Now that you have an understanding of some of the dangers of unwise spending, what should you do?

Material items rarely fix our self-image. We know deep down inside we're just followers and are afraid to be individuals. We're being led around by advertisements or peer pressure and we allow the big companies and our friends to control our thinking. Growing up involves choosing who to associate with, and trying to become your own person.

Occasionally some of your friends may pressure you to accompany them in what they want to do, even though it's something you know is not right for you. Sometimes they might try to make you feel bad if you don't go along with their plans. Those friends may be the ones you may choose to limit the amount of time you spend with them. Choosing friends carefully is kind of easy. Just avoid the ones who aren't nice to you.

Following the crowd sometimes leads to personal inner conflict, which takes away from your being happy, joyous, and free. This becomes less of an issue if you choose the right crowd to associate with. Find friends who don't need cigarettes, drugs, or alcohol to feel good about themselves. That's a good place to start. We tend to become like our friends because they think what they do is smart. An old saying that applies here is "birds of a feather flock together." If you want to see yourself clearly, it helps to look at who your friends are—you are most likely to be like them. Choose your friends wisely.

Q. How do you make new friends?
A. Just be yourself. Don't try to make people like you—most people prefer a friend who is genuine rather than a phony. Find friends that act like you would want to act and you have something good in common with such as sports, joint homework projects, or other topics that are of interest to both of you or would benefit you both.

> Try reading books like *How to Win Friends and Influence People* by Dale Carnegie.

Q. Won't my friends be jealous if I start being friends with others?
A. Maybe they will, especially if you are spending less time with them. If someone is a true friend, they'll remain your friend and support you. Explain that you choose to spend time with other people because you don't want to do certain things they take part in. They may respect you for that. They

Where Do We Go from Here?

could also become jealous and reject you. When you know you are right, stick to your path. Anyone worth having as a close friend will respect your decisions even when those decisions are not the same as theirs.

Even when people are no longer close friends they shouldn't become enemies. It's best to remain friendly even when you spend less time with them. Growing up involves choosing who to associate with, and trying to become your own person.

Becoming independent often means rejecting some of the suggestions of our parents. But we generally know they want the very best for us, so don't reject all of their advice. Their advice is not just opinions—it's usually based on life experience. Before you reject their point of view, try to understand what experience is behind what they say.

Ideally, your parents should guide you to do the right thing. Parents sometimes find it scary to raise a family. Perhaps their own parents were too busy working, or too stressed by health problems, money problems, or addiction problems to teach their children how to grow up properly. If you're not sure whether their advice is good, assume it is sound until you learn differently.

It isn't smart to do something just because someone tells you or you read it in a book, even this book. You may have to ask others and check things out to see if they are wise ideas. Your buddies may be good people but they, like all humans, aren't always right. So, where do you go?

> Find someone who has shown by their own lifestyle that they are offering their experience and not just their opinions.

Your school's guidance counsellor should have sound advice. This person has been selected by the school board because of their education and background to help people your age. The youth leader at your church may also be a big help for you. Sports teams, school bands, or some other group with whom you share a common interest are all places to develop skills that help you become your own person. Beware, not every team has a positive leader. Following directions is being a good team player. But don't allow your obedience to cross over from good to bad. Some adults may have personal agendas outside the scope of their jobs.

Do what you know or feel is right—it pays off. A conscience free of guilt helps you develop a sense of real confidence. You don't have to prove anything to peers when you feel comfortable with yourself. Your self-worth shouldn't depend on a certain style or brand name of clothes. Your self-confidence should come from within you.

Where Do We Go from Here?

Money Smart Tips for You

A book that I read many years ago is really helpful. It's called *The Richest Man in Babylon*, by George Samuel Clason. This book isn't about a fad or scheme to get rich quick. It lays down principles that will work for you today if you want to become wealthy. It takes four hours and fifty-one minutes to listen to it free online; just search audio book and the title online.

There are two rules a person can use to become wealthy, according to George Clason.

1. Ten cents out of every dollar you earn is yours to keep.
2. That is yours to keep—not to spend later.

There are many other tips in Clason's book. It works even if you owe money now.

Many people give all their money away in exchange for goods and services. They give it to the grocer, the clothing store, the telephone company, and some to … (well you get the picture). They don't keep any for themselves. If they do save any it's just the leftovers. That isn't a good plan. Place yourself first when making you financial program.

From every dollar you receive, pay yourself first. Make the others wait their turn. Don't spend your part of your income on their products. Keep that 10% for you. You're important enough for that. You deserve it! That is what saves you from worry and stress later; it leads to a secure and happy life.

Money Smarts for Teens & Twenties

You can live as well on $90 as you can on $100. All you have to do is search for things that are a better buy than you normally would have bought. Just find better buys or do without some unnecessary purchases and save that 10% for yourself.

> **Make a sport out of hunting for bargains.**

Checking different stores for better buys and uncovering less costly alternatives can be fun. It's like hunting or playing hide and seek. You don't know where the best buy is until you search it out. When you do locate a better deal than you would have gotten at the first store, it's a great feeling. It's like uncovering a prize in a treasure hunt. Just be sure you do not use your 10%—no bargain is worth that!

Postpone purchases that are not needed immediately. How important is it to have this today?

You'll never run out of money this way. If you automatically place your money in your safe place first, you make a happy life for yourself.

Saving 10% at first may not seem like much, but keep putting that 10% in a safe place. You might need help to open a bank account, but most banks or credit unions are very helpful. Watch that there are no service charges.

Look for the best deal. Don't pay any bank to hold your money. They should pay you interest. Banks use your money to invest and earn profit while they have it. That should be enough profit for them. In only two or three years you'll be amazed at how much you have saved.

Where Do We Go from Here?

You should have another account or safe place where you put another 10% of your money for unplanned emergencies and opportunities. You'll need a third place to save money for things you plan to buy in the next few months. This could be a safe place at home as long as it isn't too large an amount. Cash won't burn in a bank account—but it could if your house burns down.

You ask: What good is money if I can't spend it? Sometimes you may be tempted to take money from your savings for that special purchase. Don't do it. Here are three reasons to leave your money in your savings account.

1. When you can show a lender that you have saved money consistently, it's much easier to get a loan. If you need to start a loan, a lender will usually give you a lower interest rate on your loan if you have your own assets.

2. When you need or want money and you know you could withdraw it from your lifelong savings—don't withdraw it. Borrow it if you really must have it. Any withdrawal will have serious impact on the total future investment returns. A loan has a commitment to pay it off and will not impact your future wealth.

3. Having money gives you access to even more money. Life is much easier financially. People with no savings usually have to pay a higher rate of interest on their loans if they can even get a loan.

Money Smarts for Teens & Twenties

People will tell you it's cheaper to take your money out of your savings account than it is to pay a higher interest on a loan. Real life isn't just about math. In real life, most people rarely replace all the money they withdraw.

Just pay off the loan while still adding 10% to your own money. One day you'll have enough to be able to buy large apartment buildings or businesses if you choose. Banks will lend you enough without taking any money out of your own account.

You might begin with finding ways to really enjoy life without foolish spending. Saving money just because you should is harder to accomplish than when you enjoy doing it. Put the fun into seeking out the best deals and save your own 10% just for you. Look ahead and imagine how much easier your life will be in ten, twenty, or fifty years. Will you be able to buy a yacht or will you have to work hard to pay your monthly credit payments?

Remember, use the 10% rule sensibly but don't become too attached to money—it isn't money that is the root of all evil, it's the love of money that causes problems.

Helpful Tips

Habits formed as a teenager may last for your whole lifetime. Some of these tips may seem a nuisance to start now, but it's easier to start a new habit before you have developed

Where Do We Go from Here?

poor habits. These tips are so much easier to integrate into your daily lifestyle now before it one day costs you a fortune.

Your Vision Will Determine Your Lifestyle

Someone said typically teenagers don't plan past Friday night. In my financial planning practice, I see middle-aged people who unfortunately don't plan much further. They are the ones who are trapped in financial dilemmas.

Successful people plan further ahead. People who have shorter plans tend to be clerks and basic labourers, while those with a ten to twenty year focus rise to supervisors, managers, and business owners. People with thirty- to forty-year visions tend to be names you would recognize, like Bill Gates, Steve Jobs, and Mark Zuckerberg.

Generally, incomes roughly match an individual's life plan or vision for themselves.

Enjoy your youth. You can totally enjoy life now and still have a great future by doing some deliberate planning. Benjamin Franklin said, "If you fail to plan, you are planning to fail!"

There are so many factors involved in a life plan that it cannot be contained in one book so Like us on Facebook and follow us on Twitter.

Financial Tips

- Push the mute button on your TV remote during commercials. Advertisements are designed to get your cash.
- Quit smoking if you are a smoker. Save money on your life insurance and disability insurance premiums.

Money Smarts for Teens & Twenties

- Buy almost new cars. Depreciation on new vehicles is expensive. Hire a mechanic to examine a used car before purchasing.
- Use savings to pay your insurance annually. You can save about 8% on cost which is better than earning 2% in a savings account.
- Consider almost new items such as cars, furniture, and tools. You can save a lot compared to buying new items.
- Use Tax Free Savings Accounts for long term savings. This saves taxes without the potential downsides of RRSPs. There is no tax payable on withdrawals like there is on RRSPs.
- Don't invest in an RRSP while you are under the age of thirty-five or you have less than $35,000 to invest. Like us on Facebook or follow us on Twitter to learn about investment strategies.
- Start early: Saving $2,000 a year at 7% return from age twenty will total $689,926 at age sixty-five. Start at age thirty and it's only $330,019.
- Set up forced savings—have a withdrawal invested every payday from your account. Save 10% of all you earn for you to keep.
- Pay at least a third down for cars or appliances, pay cash for small stuff, buy a home with a mortgage.
- Abstain from using credit cards that don't get paid in full every month. Credit card interest has financially destroyed many households.
- Pay more than the minimum payment if you carry a balance on your credit card. The more you pay down, the less interest you pay.

Where Do We Go from Here?

- Don't be automatically fooled into buying RRSPs with automatic savings.
- Start an RRSP early is if your employer matches your deposits.
- Check your bank accounts monthly. Check for unfamiliar automatic debits on it. The bank may only return them up to ninety days.
- Check credit card statements to verify that all purchases are actually yours.
- Do not spend cash windfalls. Use this cash in your financial plan, not for your shopping urges.
- Start savings with your first paycheck. $1 at 7.2% doubles every ten years, so $1 will become $16 at age sixty. Start at age thirty and $1 will only be $8 age sixty. Not one penny more invested and twice the results just by starting early!
- Avoid the higher interest rates if you carry a balance on your credit cards. Credit cards offer lower interest rates with fewer rewards, or a higher interest rate with rewards points.
- Auto insurance and life insurance may cost up to 8% more to pay monthly. Your savings account pays about 1%.
- Use cash. Carry your daily allowance with you. People spend about 15% more when they use plastic to buy items.

There are three types of debt: bad, good, and better.

1. Bad debt is when you borrow money to buy something which will depreciate in value.

2. Good debt is when you borrow money to buy an asset which will appreciate in value.

3. Better debt is when you borrow money to buy assets which will appreciate in value and loan interest is tax deductible.

Money saved on expenses is not taxable. Earnings on savings accounts/investments are taxable, so 5% saved is worth more than 5% earned on investments.

Insurance Tips

- Compare rates for your life insurance and compare term to whole life. Term is cheap now but becomes extremely expensive in later years. And term insurance may expire before you expire, leaving you with no coverage at all. Life insurance companies must love term life insurance if you are one of the 50% who live past the average life expectancy. They keep your money and you have no coverage.
- Buy some whole life insurance which lasts your whole lifetime. Buy term to offset temporary needs like debts and child rearing expenses in case you die prematurely. Term life insurance is to cover temporary needs in case you die prematurely. If you live a normal life expectancy, term life may run out or become unaffordable before you die.
- Use your own term life policy instead of life insurance service charges on your mortgage, car loan, line of credit, credit cards, etc. for lower cost.
- Insure your income. The greatest asset you have is your ability to earn a living, and everything else

Where Do We Go from Here?

depends on it. Disability insurance is really important. It may cost more than life insurance but there are eight times as many foreclosures on mortgages for disability than for death.
- Start savings and life insurance with your first paycheck, but beware of RRSP loans—the interest is **not** tax deductible. RRSP loans tend to benefit the seller more frequently than the buyer.
- Don't just depend on group life insurance coverage, it's just a basic start. Generally, group life insurance is a great deal, especially if the employer is paying half. Get as much as you can. Life insurance companies make a lot of money off people who come for life insurance after they retire. If the retirees can afford the high premiums and are healthy enough to buy life insurance, fine; but most people who consult with me can't afford to buy the whole amount they want. Some get declined due to health issues which increase with age. Set up your own whole life insurance plan now.

Habits
- Drink tap water instead of bottled water. Plastics aren't always healthy containers—plus they contaminate the environment. Drinking tap water also saves you money. (*Subject to local water conditions.*)
- Get every last drop. Before you toss out "empty" plastic tubes and bottles of personal grooming products, try cutting open one side and discover how much product is left inside.

- Ride your bike to work. It feels great and you'll save on gas.
- Check online for the free audiobook, *The Richest Man in Babylon.* Listen to it. "10% of all you earn is yours to keep." Start as soon as you can
- Stop buying. A simple way to avoid bills is to stop buying anything but basics. Try it for six months. You'll be proud you did.
- Exercise and eat a healthy diet to encourage physical and mental alertness, which may help you make better financial decisions.
- Turn your unused stuff into cash by selling them at yard sales or online.
- Paint a picture or build craft items to save money on gifts. Store bought gifts may not be remembered as long as a homemade gift.
- Pay all your bills monthly. This helps you become aware of exactly where your money is going.
- Donate old clothes to the Salvation Army (or other community thrift store), and while you are there, search for bargains for yourself.
- Analyze where every penny goes for one week—then make adjustments that make sense. You alone can solve your spending problems.
- Take a thermos of coffee to work or brew coffee there. Coffee shops are expensive.
- Ask to see menus before you sit down at a restaurant. When we travelled in Europe, we found some restaurants charged twice what the bar next door did for the same item.

Where Do We Go from Here?

- Walk the dog or ride your bicycle instead of joining a fitness club. You'll save on membership dues.
- Park and walk—don't drive around looking for a parking spot. You will save gas and exercise is good for you.
- Don't use perfume. It saves you money and it won't aggravate people's allergies.
- Reduce the use of make-up to add colour to your face. Going for brisk walks could bring similar results.
- Limit manicures and pedicures for special occasions. They are costly luxuries.
- Look after your spiritual life. If you feel complete as a person you won't need to buy unnecessary consumer items to feel whole. Change your daily spending habits to change your serenity and enjoy your life. No worries.
- Don't bet or gamble. A racehorse can take a thousand people for a ride all at one time.
- Turn a hobby into a business. My friend did this with his collection of sports cards; now he travels to trade shows for fun and profit.
- Shop at a grocery store when travelling and stock up on a few snacks to take to the hotel. You'll save money.
- Drink water when you eat out. Coffee, soft drinks, or juices add up on your bill quickly.
- Don't trade freedom for credit card payments. Buying things that you don't really need costs you hours and years of labour.

Money Smarts for Teens & Twenties

Tips for Setting up Housekeeping

- Be cautious when buying groceries. Sometimes the bigger container is **not** as cheap as the average size package or can. Usually the most commonly used size is the better price in supermarkets. The small size is usually costs more also. Bring a calculator when grocery shopping to compare value of sizes.
- Don't buy or cook more food than you need. Think before you buy.
- Coupons and websites can be great tools for saving money.
- When shopping for an item you want, don't search through aisles of stuff you don't want. Ask a clerk for directions. This prevents you from buying things you don't need.
- Host a cooking party. Get friends to compete for the cheapest, tastiest, healthiest, quickest dishes to prepare. Have fun and learn new easy recipes. Save money too.
- If your freezer isn't full, fill plastic bags with water and freeze. A full freezer costs less to run.

Where Do We Go from Here?

Check our Like us on Facebook or follow us on Twitter for more tips and Q & A.

Your comments and questions would be appreciated. You can email me at ghughes@nb.aibn.com

Also check Smart Choice Life Inc or Youth Advantage Project for Culture Inc for additional information.

About the Author

Gordon Hughes CFP became a financial planner in 1991. Previously he worked in Banking and Credit Management but felt he could better serve people as an advisor. Gordon earned designations in credit management, lifestyle planning and financial planning. In 2009 he incorporated his own life insurance and investment sales company. Smart Choice Life Inc. brokers products from 20 Life Insurance companies and banks to offer products better suited to their clients. They work for their clients – not a company.

In 2011, a year after his son Greg died Gordon and his two daughters started a scholarship program in Greg's honour to assist children of low income families to enroll in music, art, dance or acting programs. The company is the 'Youth Advantage Project for Culture Inc'.

Money Smarts for Teens & Twenties

Gordon has authored a financial advice column in The Daily Gleaner in Fredericton NB. His weekly column shared actual mistakes people made and suggestions to help others avoid those pitfalls. He didn't regurgitate commonly held beliefs; he used real life circumstances and doable solutions.

His predictions have been surprisingly accurate. In 1998 when interest rates were around 7% he predicted that we would see 2% GIC rates within 5 years. He recommended that seniors purchase life annuities before the interest rates declined. Hindsight affirms that was a wise investment choice for many.

Another prediction in 1998 was that we would see 20% 30% even 40% growth followed by a 50% drop. In 2000 the Toronto stock exchange was at 11,000 and dropped to less than 6,000 by 2002.

Basically similar results repeated growth in 2005, 2006, 2007, and a drop in 2008. He won recognition prizes for his work for moving clients and prospects into productive investments which are safer than mutual funds and protected them from a huge drop in 2008.

Gordon welcomes inquiries. Call 506 454-3346 or email Gordon@SmartChoiceLife.com

CPSIA information can be obtained
at www.ICGtesting.com
Printed in the USA
LVHW090501100420
652925LV00004B/13